VICTORIA

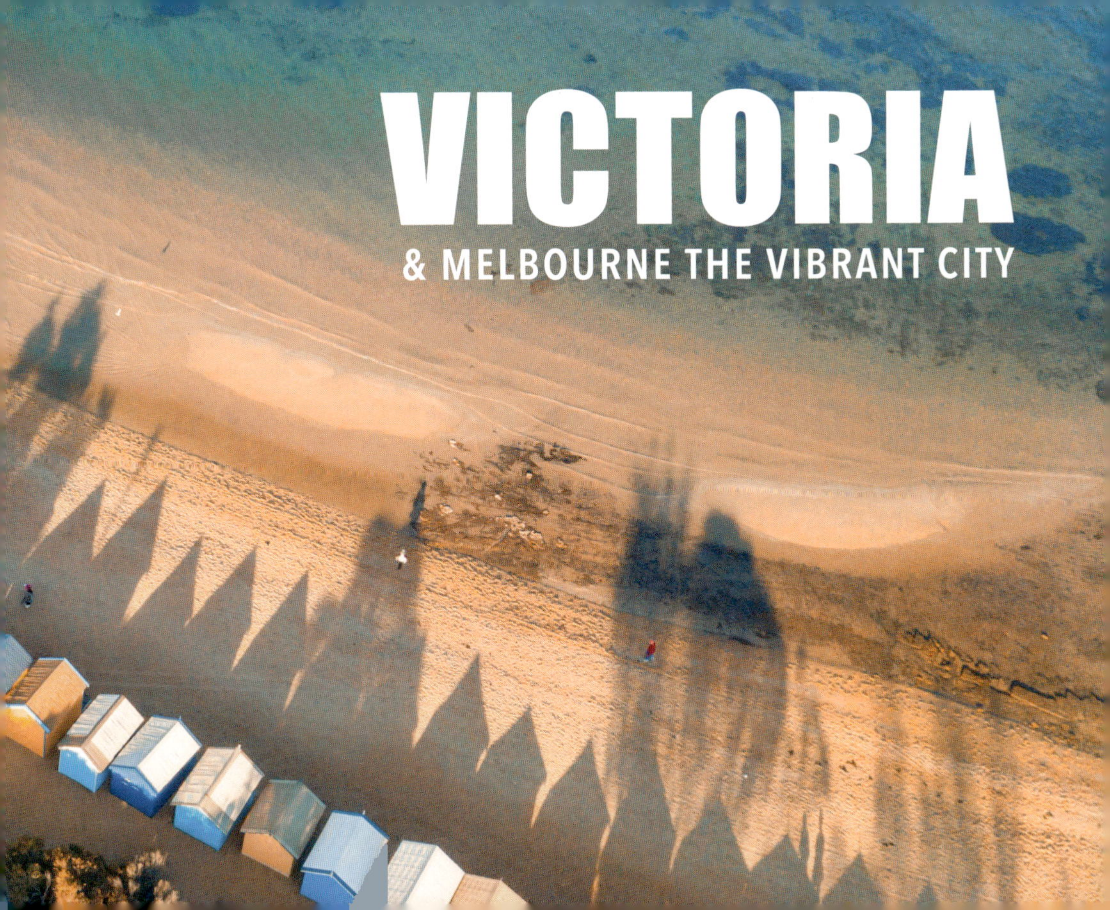

VICTORIA

& MELBOURNE THE VIBRANT CITY

INTRODUCTION

Victoria is bordered to the west by South Australia and to the north by New South Wales. The northern border follows the squiggly course of the Murray River from the South Australian border to where the Murray actually starts, before making a southeast beeline to the coast. To the south of Victoria is the Tasman Sea, separating Victoria from Tasmania. Victoria is Australia's smallest mainland state, at 237,659 square kilometres.

Victoria produces a third of all of Australia's apples, close to 20 million sheep and their lambs graze Victorian grasslands, so there are three sheep to every person. Victoria is almost literally Australia's land of milk and honey. Almost one-third of all Australian beekeepers live in Victoria and the state accounts for a whopping two-thirds of the nation's milk.

Victoria has a public holiday for a horse race, named the Melbourne Cup and

Apollo Bay and Barham paradise scenic reserve along the Great Ocean Road.

has many sporting events, including the Formula One Australian Grand Prix, Australian Open Tennis, and they are passionate about AFL.

Victoria boasts beautiful coastal drives with a foodie culture of sensational food and wine using local ingredients to the state featuring lots of wineries in the regional areas of Victoria, stunning mountains and national parks as well as surfing beaches including the famous Bells Beach where they host the Rip Curl Pro (formerly Bells Beach Surf Classic).

Victoria offers it all, as well as many beautiful drives along the coast of Victoria taking in the Great Ocean Road, and Phillip Island, just south of Melbourne is home to Little Penguins to the Yarra Valley.

Victoria was named after Queen Victoria and Melbourne is the city with the highest population of Greeks outside of Greece.

Melbourne has many cultural institutions such as the stunning building which homes the State Library of Victoria, The Melbourne Museum, The Royal Botanic Gardens, National Gallery of Victoria and the Royal Exhibition Building.

Melbourne is a city of wide streets, boulevards and avenues, except in the centre where it's a fascinating complex of small streets and lanes with all sorts of treasures waiting to be discovered by the persistent visitor who's prepared to do a lot of walking.

It's an eclectic city, with a vibrant cafe and restaurant culture. Melburnians visit more cafes per capita than anyone else in Australia – almost two-thirds of the population are regular cafe customers.

Chinatown in Melbourne is one of the best districts for food in the world

with Chinese settlement dating back to the mid 1800s where immigrants from Hong Kong came to Victoria on their way to the gold fields during the gold rush a significant period in Victorian history.

Creative people flock to Melbourne to exchange art and ideas in the great indoors. The city also comes with sense of humor, the centre of Australian comedy.

Melbourne is considered one of the world's leading livable cities. Also part of the edgy and creative side of Melbourne is the street art on the sides of buildings which gives Melbourne the title for most vibrant and cultural city of Australia with more than 250 kilometres of tram tracks.

UniSuper
AFLOAT

THE CITY OF MELBOURNE

FLINDERS STREET STATION

A cultural icon of Australia, Flinders Street Station in Melbourne is the oldest train station in all of Australia, having been established in 1854.

It is an iconic landmark of the city, characterised by its notable green copper dome, yellow facade, arched entrance, tower, and clocks. The station spans more than two city blocks east of Swanston Street, nearly reaching Market Street and backing onto the Yarra River.

With 13 platforms and various structures, Flinders Street Station is a bustling hub in the heart of Melbourne's central business district. Its main building, completed in 1909, is a cultural symbol of Melbourne and a must-see destination for visitors to the city.

Today, heritage-listed Flinders Street Station is the one of the busiest suburban railway stations in the Southern Hemisphere and the railway station sits on the edge of Flinders and Swanston Streets.

The clock displays under the main dome, indicating the departing times of the next trains, have been around since the 1860s.

Due to increasing demand, Flinders Street Station's development became necessary at the turn of the 20th century and the railway commissioners advertised a competition for a new and improved station, offering a prize of 500 pounds to the winner.

J.W. Fawcett and H.P.C. Ashworth were the winning designers of the station that remains standing today. It took 10 years to complete the entire reconstruction of the station, which cost approximately £514,000.

Flinders Street Station.

Shrine of Remembrance.

State Library Victoria.

State Library Victoria.

333 Collins Street was formerly the Commercial Bank of Australia.

Melbourne Central Shot Tower view from under the glass dome.

Gog and Magog and Gaunt's clock at the Royal Arcade.

Royal Arcade.

Chadstone Shopping Centre.

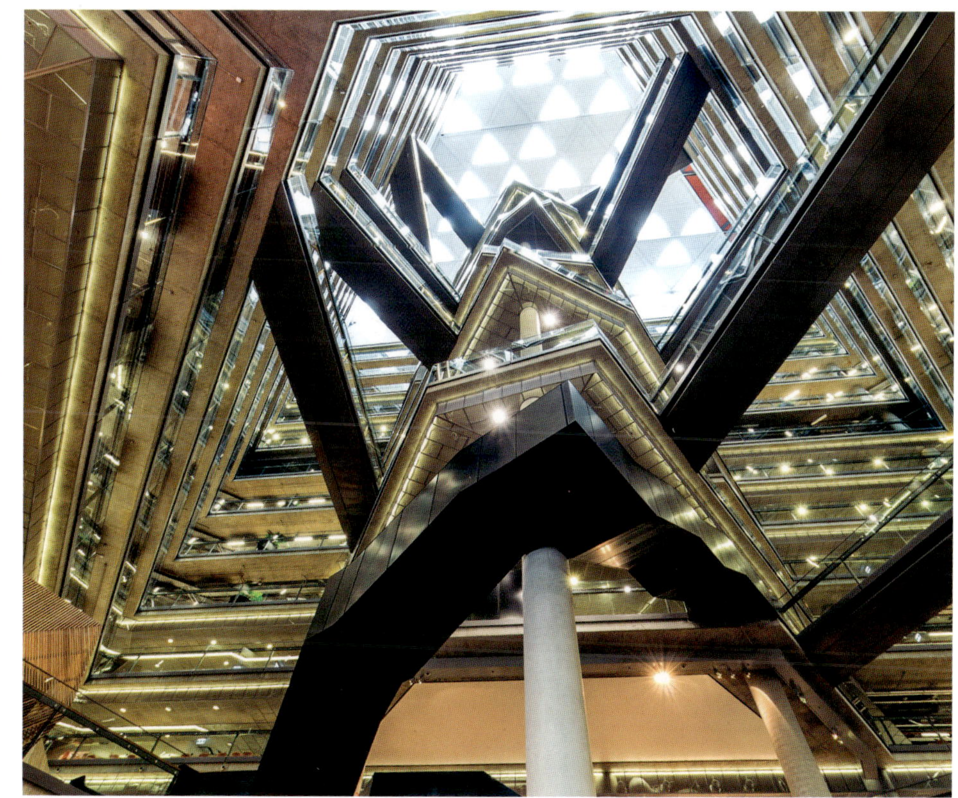

Interior atrium of the National Australia Bank offices at 700 Bou-ke Street, Docklands.

Flinders Street Railway Station and St Paul's Cathedral.

Interior of St Paul's Cathedral.

Royal Exhibition Building.

Royal Exhibition Building.

SEA LIFE Melbourne Aquarium.

SEA LIFE

Fitzroy Gardens – located just east of the C3D.

Royal Botanic Gardens.

Royal Botanic Gardens floral clock.

Royal Botanic Gardens.

A GOLDEN AGE
of CHINA

ONAL GALLERY OF VICTORIA

Parliament House.

Immigration Museum.

Federation Square.

arintji

acmi
WONDERLAND

ACMI – Federation Square.

Queen Victoria Market, officially opened in 1878.

Queen Victoria
MARKET
KEEP LEFT

Victoria Barracks Museum.

Melbourne Skydeck.

Melbourne Observatory.

Captain Cook's Cottage in Fitzroy Garden

Captain Cook's Cottage in Fitzroy Garder

Tram in Melbourne CBD.

ANZ
2087
yarra trams

CITY CIRCLE
City Circle
866

Y CIRCLE TRAM
MELBOURNE

Arts Centre Melbourne.

Footbridge over the Yarra River at Melbourne Convention and Exhibition Centre (MCEC).

Melbourne Cricket Ground and the Australian Sports Museum.

Melbourne CBD at night.

Webb Bridge, Docklands.

KIA
Emirates
FLY BETTER

Australian Open at Melbourne Park.

Melbourne skyline featuring the MCG.

Melbourne Cricket Ground (MCG).

Old Melbourne Gaol.

Old Melbourne Gaol.

Old Melbourne Gaol.

Luna Park Melbourne.

Old Treasury Building.

Melbourne Zoo.

Melbourne skyline.

Melbourne skyline from Yarra River.

Melbourne city and the Yarra River.

Flinders Street Station on the Yarra River.

AAMI Park, the Melbourne Rectangular Stacium.

Flemington Racecourse where the famous Melbourne Cup race takes place.

Docklands.

Near the banks of the Yarra River.

Melbourne CBD laneway.

CHINATOWN

Chinatown, a renowned area in Melbourne, has a fascinating history that dates back to the gold rush era of the 1850s.

It is the longest continuous Chinese settlement in the western world, with its central focus being Little Bourke Street. The alleys that interconnect Chinatown to Bourke Street and Lonsdale Street are also well-known landmarks. Follow the glowing lanterns to the Chinese Museum and marvel at the winding Chinese dragons. For an incredible lunchtime experience, try the yum cha, fried pork mini buns or fried chicken and prawn dumplings.

Explore the area's quirky arcades and hidden bars, and discover the many restaurants in the lanes and alleyways.

墨爾本唐人街

北京烤鴨店
Da Hu
CHINESE
RESTAURANT
PEKING
DUCK
7 ELEVEN
TEASER | 奉茶
Russell St
24 HOURS

EXFORD HOTEL
EXFORD HOTEL
Jin dumpling & noodle house
ONE WAY
TANGO LESSONS
BLUES SUNDAYS
LIVE SPORTS
BOTTLE SHOP

Street art.

Temple of Boom outdoor exhibition.

Crown Melbourne.

Gayip sculpture along the Yarra River at Southbank.

The LUME multimedia exhibition 'Monet and Friends'.

Angel sculpture by Deborah Halpern, Birrarung Marr park by the banks of the Yarra River.

Melbourne tram.

Southbank.

Laneways in Melbourne CBD.

Lygon Street in the suburb of Carlton.

sea Salt
Goldhar Pl
P
40
40

Albert Park F1 Grand Prix circuit.

Australian Grand Prix at Albert Park.

Albert Park.

Melbourne Planetarium (Scienceworks).

Scienceworks (Museums Victoria).

Princes Pier - Port Melbourne

THE BEACHES, COASTLINES AND BAYS

Parks

Marina Melbourne.

Brighton Beach

Brighton Beach.

Brighton Beach.

Brighton Beach pier.

St Kilda.

Palais Theatre, St Kilda.

St Kilda Pier.

St Kilda.

Sandringham.

Frankston Pier.

Frankston Pier.

Flinders Pier, Mornington Peninsula.

Flinders Pier, Mornington Peninsula.

Mornington Peninsula.

Barwon Heads.

Barwon River Beach and Barwon Heads Bridge.

Geelong.

Geelong.

Geelong bay walk. Sculpture by Jan Mitchell.

Marlo township and the Snowy River.

GREAT OCEAN ROAD

GREAT OCEAN ROAD

The Great Ocean Road, a 240-kilometre road along the southeastern coast of Australia, is a National Heritage-listed site that connects the Victorian cities of Torquay and Allansford.

Along this route, you can spot native Australian fauna such as koalas, kangaroos and whales.

Additionally, you can zipline through a treetop canopy, climb to the peak of a volcanic crater and enjoy regional dining on a cliff or by the beach. Make sure to stop and take in the stunning views and keep an eye out for wildlife.

This road is known for its breathtaking scenery and is considered one of the most stunning driving routes in the world.

The Great Ocean Road hugs the coastline, passes through the rainforest, and cuts through quaint towns, offering not only incredible views, but also a variety of action-packed adventures and activities.

The journey begins in Torquay and ends in Allansford. It's important to note that only eight apostles remain today.

Twelve Apostles

London Bridge, a famous rock arch in the Port Campbell National Park.

Split Point Lighthouse.

Great Ocean Road viewed from Teddy's Lookout.

Loch Ard Gorge rock formations located along the Great Ocean Road.

The London Arch, formerly London Bridge when it was a double span, offshore natural bridge until the span closer to land collapsed in 1990.

GREAT

EAN ROAD
HISTORICAL
MARKER

Great Ocean Road.

The Grotto.

Anglesea township and Point Roadknight headland.

Apollo Bay panoramic aerial view from Mariners lookout.

Bells Beach.

Surfers at Bells Beach.

Bells Beach on a summer morning.

The historic Proudfoots Boatshed on the Hopkins River.

Middle Island and Merri Island, Warrnambool.

The rocky coastline at Loutitt Bay, Lorne.

Devil's Elbow between Fairhaven and Lorne.

Bay of Islands, Peterborough.

Kennett River park.

Airey's Inlet cliffs with lighthouse.

Port Fairy.

Point Nepean and Port Phillip Bay.

Hopkins River and Warrnambool.

Great Ocean Road.

Great Ocean Road private home on the hillside.

Mutton Bird Island arches.

Mt Buller, Mansfield.

COUNTRY VICTORIA

Beechworth.

Beechworth Post Office.

Craig's Hut (as seen in *The Man from Snowy River* movie) in the Victorian Alps.

Mt Buller and the Victorian Alps.

Southside

Mt Buller.

Ovens Valley from the lookout on top of Mount Buffalo, Bright.

Yarra Valley wine barrels.

Yarra Valley.

Mt Arapiles.

Apple and cherry orchard at Seville Hill Winery, Seville.

Sheep at the foot of the Grampians Ranges near Dunkeld.

Cows in a paddock near Marysville in the Shire of Murrindindi.

-AFP

Yarra Valley.

Beechworth Court House.

Ned Kelly, Glenrowan.

Murray River with motor traffic bridge to Mildura.

Paddle boats on the Murray River, Echuca.

Echuca.

Echuca paddle steamer.

Horseshoe Lagoon Nature Reserve, part of Moama's Wetland and Floodplain Reserve.

Port of Echuca.

Horsham.

Giant Koala,
Dadswells Bridge.

The Cosmopolitan Hotel, built in 1866, Trentham.

Trentham Falls, Dayesford Ballarat.

Castlemaine.

Kangaroo Hotel, Maldon.

Maldon Railway Station.

DANGER
DO NOT
CLIMB

Bendigo.

Bendigo Chinese Gardens Reserve.

Bendigo.

Bendigo tramways depot.

Sovereign Hill, Ballarat.

Sovereign Hill, Ballarat.

Church in Ballarat.

Kryal Castle, a replica medieval village near Ballarat.

Ballarat Town Centre.

THE SPORTING GLOBE®
THE SPORTING
40
AREA
Heineken
Heineken

Kyneton.

Maryborough's historic grandstand.

The Big Wine Bottle, Rutherglen.

Old winery building near Rutherglen.

The historic Soldiers' Memorial Hall (built 1927) in Rutherglen.

Warburton Swing 3ridge in Warburton.

The historic Grand Hotel, Mildura.

Rio Vista historic building, Mildura.

Clunes Town Hall.

Historic gold town of Clunes.

Canola fields inbetween Smeaton and Clunes in the Victorian goldfields.

Walhalla Fire Station in the small Gippsland town of Walhalla.

Walhalla town.

Minyip.

Warracknabeal Post Office.

Puffing Billy

Puffing Billy Railway.

Gembrook Station of Puffing Billy Railway.

Dandenong Ranges National Park.

Dandenong Ranges.

Dandenong Ranges forest.

Alfred Nicholas Gardens in Sherbrooke.

Hanging Rock.

A volcanic group of rocks atop a hill in the Macedon Ranges.

Hang ng Rock.

Mount Martha on the Mornington Peninsula.

The boardwalk at Mount Martha.

Scenic river in Victoria.

Swan Hill.

Post Office at the Swan Hill Pioneer Settlement.

Swan Hill Church.

Rustic silo.

Old metal silo near a dam, central Victoria.

Murray River.

NATURE

Lake Wendouree.

Grampians National Park.

McKenzie Falls in the Grampians National Park.

View from the Boroka Lookout in the Grampians National Park.

Mt Hotham.

Mt Bogong, the highest peak in the Victorian alps.

Mt Feathertop near Mt Hotham.

View of The Horn formation near The Hump at Mt Buffalo.

View from Pinnacle Lookout in Grampians National Park.

Victoria Park Lake, Shepparton.

Mt Arapiles.

Redwood Forest,
Warburton.

Rainforest Gallery on the slopes of Mt Donna Buang near Warburton.

Great Otway National Park.

Great Otway National Park.

Tree top walk at the Great Otway National Park.

Hopetoun Falls in the Great Otway National Park.

Cohuna.

Salt deposits on shores of Lake Tyrrell.

Loch Lel pink salt lake, Dimboola.

Mt Arapiles.

Wallagaraugh River at Mallacoota.

Goulburn River valley near Alexandra.

Grampians National Park mountain range.

Lake Hume near Albury.

Regional Victoria highlands.

WILDLIFE

Major Mitchell's Cockatoo.

Orange-bellied Parrot

Scarlet Honeyeater.

Welcome Swallows.

Australian Hobby.

Rainbow Lorikeet.

Rainbow Bee-eater.

Long-billed Corella.

Rose Robin.

Australian Owlet-nightjar.

Rainbow Lorikeet.

Red-rumped Parrot.

Sharp-tailed Sandpiper.

King Parrot.

Gang-gang Cockatoo.

Red-tailed Black Cockatoo.

New Holland Honeyeater

Southern Right Whale.

Humpback Whale.

Kookaburra.

Great Cormorant.

Australian Fur Seal.

Fairy Penguin.

A pod of bottlenose Burrunan dolphins

Stingray

Cone shell.

Wedge-tailed Shearwater.

Bilby.

Yellow-footed Rock-wallaby.

Koala.

Platypus.

Wombat.

Common Brushtail Possum.

Grey-headed Flying-Fox.

Powerful Owl.

Highlands Copperhead.

Golden Stag Beetle.

Chequered Cuckoo Bee.

Orange-thighed Frog.

Needlebush.

Wild emu at Tower Hill Wildlife Reserve.

Cape Barren Goose.

Emerald Dove.

Lace Monitor.

Long-necked Turtle

White-necked Heron

Brolga.

Grey Kangaroo.

First published in 2024 by New Holland Publishers
Sydney

Level 1, 178 Fox Valley Road, Wahroonga, NSW 2076, Australia

newhollandpublishers.com

A record of this book is held at the National Library of Australia.

ISBN 9781760796617

Managing Director: Fiona Schultz
Designer: Andrew Davies
Production Director: Arlene Gippert
Printed in China

10 9 8 7 6 5 4 3 2 1

Keep up with New Holland Publishers:

NewHollandPublishers

@newhollandpublishers

H-AFP